Charlie Chaplin

ANNUAL

BROWN, WATSON

Printed in Holland.

I.S.B.N. 7027 0040 1

Brown Watson Ltd.,
30-34 Langham Street,
London,
W1N 5LB.

80 P.

THE LIFE & TIMES of Charlie Chaplin

It is unlikely that Charlie Chaplin as a youngster ever expected to be such a famous comedian. Most of his early life was spent in dire poverty . . . In his autobiography Charlie reveals many of the tragic incidents that veiled his early life.

He was born on April 16th 1889 in East Lane, Walworth, London. His mother supported him and his elder brother Sydney by singing in Vaudeville and at that time they lived reasonably well . . .

But when Charlie was five his mother lost her voice and was forced to retire from the stage. From this one unfortunate blow the Chaplin family travelled from one slum house to another. Often literally starving hungry, the brothers would go in search of some menial task in order to earn a few pennies. Because Mrs Chaplin rarely ate she grew ill and incapable of looking after her two sons.

Subsequently, Charlie and Sydney were taken to a workhouse where they spent many miserable months. As soon as she could, Mrs. Chaplin collected Charlie and Sydney from the dismal abode, but tragedy struck the household again when Mrs Chaplin suffered a nervous breakdown and was sent to Cane Hill Lunatic Asylum, never to fully recover from her illness.

When Charlie was nine he joined his first troupe called The Eight Lancashire Lads. During this period Charlie met many memorable performers, whom he mentions in his book.

Of the many artists Charlie saw as a child, it wasn't necessarily the successful ones who impressed him. No, he preferred the ones who possessed unique personalities off stage. For example, Zarmo the comedy tramp juggler. Every morning, and as soon as the theatre opened, he would commence practising. One of his special tricks was to balance a billiard cue on his chin, then throw a billiard ball up and catch it on the end of the cue. Then would you believe, he would toss another ball into the air and attempt to catch it on the top of the first . . . something he didn't do very often. However, he intended to try it out for the first time on the audience. There was an expectant hush in the wings as Zarmo began the trick. Quite amazingly it worked first time but only brought mild applause from the audience. The manager told Zarmo the reason was that he should have made the trick look more difficult.

Film: Shoulder Arms

Hynkel, the Great Dictator (Charles Chaplin), and his side, have to endure the rantings of Napoloni, Dictator of Bacteria (Jack Oakie).

The Jewish barber (Charles Chaplin) impersonates the Great Dictator. Produced, written and directed by Charles Chaplin. "The Great Dictator" stars Charles Chaplin, Paulette Goddard and Jack Oakie.

Far right Film: Shoulder Arms

Zarmo's answer to that was that he wasn't expert enough to miss it yet.

Another funny and strange act Chaplin raved about were two trapeze clowns who, as they both swung from the trapeze, would ferociously kick each other in the face with large padded shoes. "Ouch"! said the victim. "I dare you to do that again!"

"Do yer?" . . . Bang! And the recipient would look surprised and groggy and say: "He did do it again!" To Chaplin it seemed a strange way for brothers to act, yet off stage they were devoted to one another.

After a spell with the Eight Lancashires Charlie drifted around doing odd jobs . . . He was a news vendor, printer, toy-maker, glass-blower, doctor's boy and he even sold flowers outside his local pub, a lucrative business until his mother found out!

During this period Charlie never lost sight of his ultimate dream, to be an actor.

He had his first real break at twelve when

Film: City Lights

he played a role in "Jim, The Romance of a Cockney." For this Charlie earned a princely two pounds fifty pence.

He was a success and was later offered the part of Billie in the stage show of Sherlock Holmes. After a couple of years playing the suburbs, Charlie's brother introduced him to Fred Karno, who eventually signed him up.

When Chaplin felt he had reached the limit of his prospects in England he joined the Karno Company in America.

Mack Sennett had first seen Charlie when he was playing a drunk in "A Night In An English Music Hall" with Karno's Company, touring the States and Canada. Sennett said that if he ever became a big shot, (at that time Sennett was working as a five dollar a day extra for D. W. Griffith in the Biograph Company) he would sign up Chaplin.

It was in Philadelphia where Charlie was playing on his second tour of America, that a telegram arrived for the company manager.

"I wonder if this means you," the manager said to Chaplin. The telegram read: IS THERE A MAN CALLED CHAFFIN IN YOUR COMPANY OR SOMETHING LIKE THAT . . . STOP . . . IF SO WILL HE COMMUNICATE WITH KESSELL AND BAUMAN.

Chaplin thought he had been left a fortune by a rich old aunt—actually it was Sennett's offer of a contract to work for the famous Keystone Comedies.

Chaplin's first film was called "Making A Living", considered by most to be a second rate movie . . . The follow up "Kid Auto Races In Venice", a five minute film, proved that Charlie had real acting ability.

For the part Charlie borrowed a pair of huge trousers and a rather small bowler hat from Fatty Arbuckle. The enormous shoes, with their long, curled up toes were lent by another fellow comedian.

Charlie didn't know it at the time but this crazy outfit was to gain him worldwide fame.

"Kid Auto Races" had no real story and certainly no script . . . Charlie was told to go out in front of the camera and be funny.

The film showed the comic clown getting in the way of the camera which was taking pictures of the children's auto race.

As the kids passed, Charlie would explode into gales of laughter . . . much to the amazement of the straight faced crowd.

The stunning outcome of this short film was that although Chaplin had only appeared briefly he had managed to cram in the full richness of his humour and make an important impact.

"Mabel's Strange Predicament" was Chaplin's third film, the one that really began to make people sit up and ask who he was. In the movie Charlie played a hotel gate-crasher who chases people around hotel rooms, through windows and onto balconies. Charlie's delightful mannerisms started to shine through. The absurd gestures began to appear, like the scene in a hotel lobby where our little tramp tripped over a lady's foot and raised his hat to apologise, then tripped over a bucket and did the hat routine again.

After the showing of "Mabel's Strange Predicament" Charlie was stopped by a fellow actor who told him: "Boy, you've really started something." It was after he had seen the reaction from the crowd and the response he received from his fellow actors that Charlie decided to stick with his costume and zany walk at all costs!

During one year at Keystone, Chaplin made

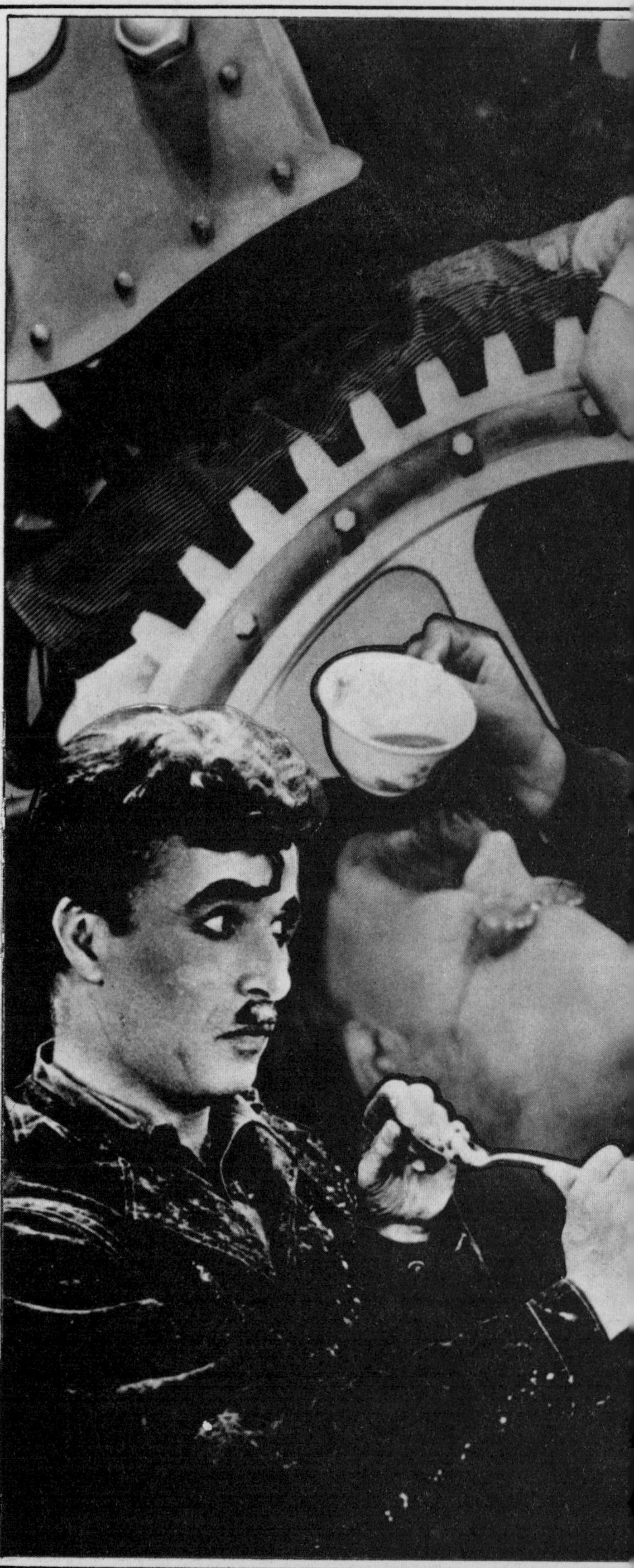

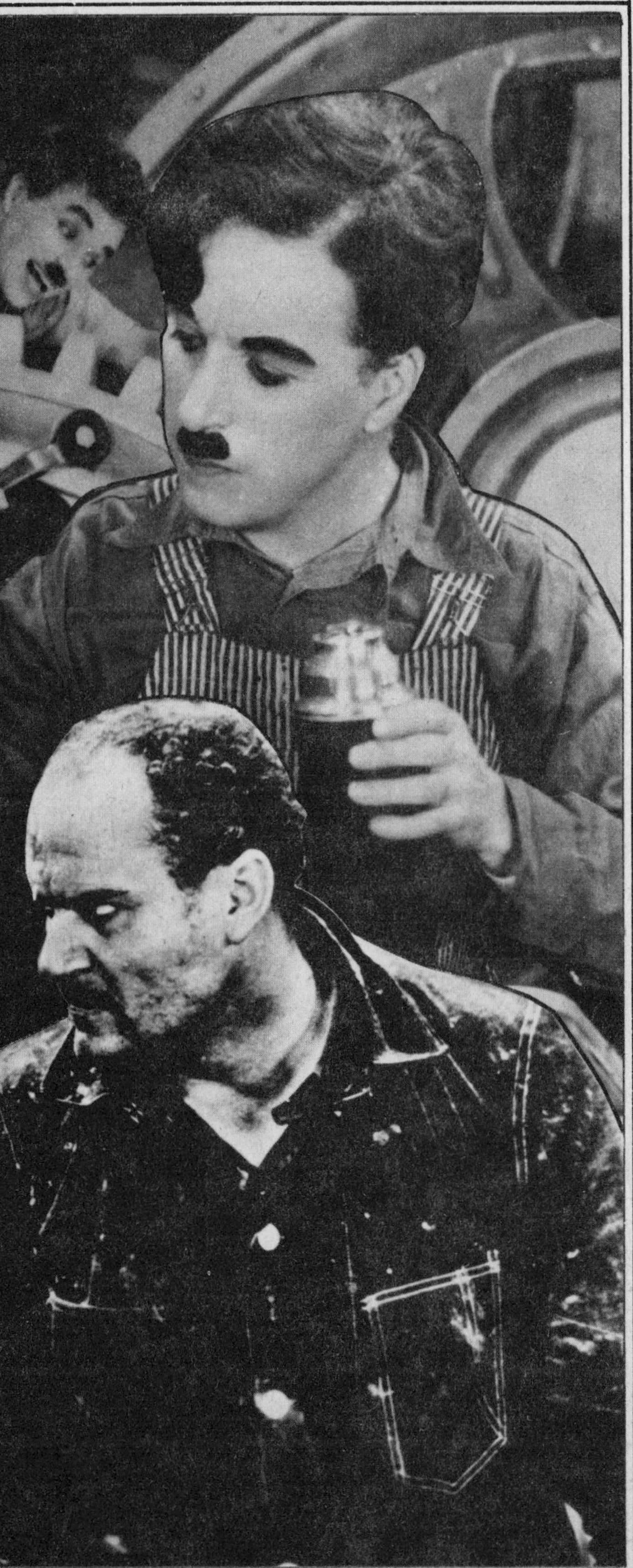

Scenes from Modern Times

thirty-five movies. In "Mabel At The Wheel" he wore his ancient costume from his very first film, which consisted of an old frock coat, a top hat and drooping moustache. In "His Musical Career", Charlie played a piano mover, who dragged the wrong pianos up and down streets and stairs and finally into a lake.

In "Laughing Gas", a particularly funny picture, Chaplin played a stooge to Doctor Pain, a dentist. Throughout the farce Charlie innocently went around the waiting room terrifying the patients—and in an endeavour to wake one man he taps him on the head with a mallet!

Most Keystone movies took no more than a week to make and in fact Charlie actually produced "Twenty Minutes of Love" in an afternoon.

In most of Chaplin's early films he played a likeable 'bad guy'. He could make the audience believe he was a polo-player, a musician or a scientist. However in other films he wasn't above picking up cigarette butts or robbing a baby of its candy. Chaplin's films usually depicted a sort of love hate relationship with babies and in "His Trysting Place" he proved the point . . . He would yank up the baby by the scruff of its pants in a famously untender manner. Of the thirty-five movies he made in that first year, Charlie directed twenty-two of them himself. His inspiration came from real incidents like the day he heard there was a flood down on main street . . . Charlie and his crew rushed to the scene and used it as a back-cloth to their film.

Although Charlie could cause gales of laughter with buckets, custard pies and all sorts of enemies and allies—it wasn't until he made "The New Janitor" that he realised he could also make people cry! After the movie, which was supposed to be a comedy, an actress was asked by Chaplin why she was crying and she said: "I know it is supposed to be funny, but you just make me weep."

In "The Tramp", Charlie played himself, no longer a piano mover, butcher or baker but a free wheeling vagabond.

Charlie the tramp saves Edna, a farmer's daughter, from thieves. Charlie is wounded by them, the daughter nurses him back to health. Eventually Edna's husband returns, and our poor little hobo is forced to pack his bundle and set off down the long road into the distance.

When Chaplin changed film companies his style altered a little, although there were still

Charlie in the famous scene from the film 'Gold Rush', where starving he satisfies his appetite by eating his boiled boot.

many memorable Keystone moments, like the scene in which Charlie pumps a cow's tail up and down to get milk and another funny sequence when he falls down a flight of stairs and lands the right way up, still calmly smoking his cigarette. There was also the never to be forgotten scene where Charlie hung his hat on his shoe to hastily cover a hole in the sole.

At his new film company Charlie made thirteen films. One of the most interesting was the hectic, high speed movie "Work". In it Charlie plays a paperhanger/decorator—he does everything with the paper except stick it and of course the paste ends up on his boss's head. Charlie, in an attempt to make amends douses the poor man with water, and the mucky twosome end up slithering incapably about in the mess! Bored with the whole business, Charlie then picks up the decorator's tools and starts to manicure his hands with them! Filing his nails with a foot long file, cleaning his fingers with a trowel and buffing them with the enormous polisher.

These were the moments the audiences held precious . . . His comic inventiveness has always been prized, like the dismembering of the clock in "The Pawnshop" or the delicately eaten meal of stewed boots with spaghetti-like laces in "Gold Rush" . . . all employ touches of genius.

When Chaplin eventually joined First National Films his output had dropped. During 1918-19 he made three films, "A Dog's Life", "Shoulder Arms" and "Sunnyside".

"A Dog's Life" depicted Charlie as a tramp who roamed the countryside with his dog, originally rescued from a fight with a pack of other hounds. Together they lived "A Dog's Life".

After nine more movies with First National Chaplin formed his own company called United Artists, with Douglas Fairbanks and made among other movies "The Circus", "City Lights" and "Limelight".

Although Charlie didn't live like a beggar when he became famous . . . he certainly knew what the condition was like. The embarrassment of having no money and the agony of being laughed at for wearing his mother's cut down tights to school had left their mark and of course he would never forget his days in the workhouse. It's perhaps movie justice that his portrayal of a tramp eventually brought him immense success and fortune!

The End

Charlie knew Mr. Winklepin would be a pain in the neck from the first moment he met him.

Charlie hadn't seen his Aunt Rosie for several years, and he had a pleasant surprise when he bumped into her in Uptown High Street one day.

"Well, fancy seeing you, Auntie!" exclaimed Charlie. "What are you doing here in Uptown?"

"I live here," Auntie replied. "I've got a little house round the corner. Come and see, and have a cup of tea."

So Charlie accepted the invitation. He intended to stay for only an hour, but actually he stayed for nearly a week. And it was all due to a silly twerp who suffered under the name of Walter Winklepin.

Just when Charlie and his aunt were seated enjoying tea, the door flew open and something copped Charlie a fourpenny-one in the back of the neck.

"Eeowch!" wailed Charlie.

"Oh Mr. Winklepin, please be careful with your trombone!" exclaimed Auntie in upset tones. "He's such a wonderful musician, you know," she added by way of explanation to Charlie. "He's never without his instrument."

"Don't apologise for me!" retorted Walter rudely. "If he puts his silly fat head in the way, that's his fault! Where's my tea?" he added.

Without even a nod of recognition—or a word of apology for biffing Chas in the neck with his trombone—Walter Winklepin sat down at the tea table and proceeded to scoff everything he could lay his hands on.

"What a proper pain-in-the-neck!" thought Charlie to himself. "If he's Auntie's lodger she ought to lodge a complaint and get rid of the twerp!"

Charlie soon discovered that Auntie had many more reasons for wishing herself rid of Walter Winklepin.

He imagined himself to be a first-class trombone-player. As soon as tea was finished he went up to his room, and within a few minutes a horrible headache-making noise disturbed the peace of Auntie Rosie's parlour.

"Gosh! You don't put up with *that*, do you, Auntie?" gasped Charlie, flinching.

His aunt looked worried.

"I—I'm afraid I have to let Mr. Winklepin practise in his room, Charlie," she said, shouting to make herself heard above the row. "He refuses to be spoken to about it. And Mr. Belltupp, the landlord, is worrying me, too," she added.

"What is the landlord worried about, Auntie?" Charlie enquired. "If you're behind with the rent, I can help you."

"Oh, no it isn't that," Auntie said. "Mr. Belltupp is always complaining about the noise that comes from this house. He says it disturbs his other tenants in the houses on either side of mine. And he says it will have to stop or he will have to turn me out!"

Thanks to a ventriloquist's telephone trick, Winklepin would soon be on the receiving end of Charlie's prank.

Charlie frowned. He couldn't have his kind old auntie worried like this.

"I'll pop up and have a word with Winklepin, Auntie," said Charlie, getting out of his chair and moving to the door. "Don't worry—I won't annoy him," he added, seeing Auntie's look of anxiety. "I'll just talk to him as man to man."

The trouble was that Walter Winklepin wasn't a *man*. He was a conceited kind of twit. Charlie had already reckoned he was a pain-in-the-neck. As soon as he stepped into the lodger's room Charlie had ample proof that Winklepin was also a pain-in-the-nose! B O N K!

That was the end of the push-out part of his trombone clonking Charlie on the nose!

"Owch!" yelped our hero. "Mind what you're doing!"

"And you mind your own business!" snarled Walter Winklepin, brandishing the long musical instrument threateningly. "If you've come up here from that old faggot to yap about the noise, you're wasting your time —and mine! Buzz off!"

"What you don't seem to understand is that if you continue to make a noisy nuisance of yourself, my Auntie Rosie will be turned out of her house by the landlord!" retorted Charlie. "And that means out you go, too!"

"Don't try to scare me!" sneered Winklepin. "She can bribe the landlord by doubling the rent. Ha, ha! Then he won't turn her out."

Charlie could see that no amount of talking would make the nasty lodger see sense and be reasonable. So Charlie went downstairs again to his aunt to report failure.

"I knew it would be no use," sighed Auntie, sadly. "There's nothing you can do, Charlie."

But Charlie didn't agree. He had already got a bright idea sizzling in his head, and that evening he treated himself to a visit to the local Variety Theatre.

He had already read an advertisement in the local paper which said that a world-famous Variety star known as 'Vicky the Ventriloquist' was to appear at the local theatre that night. And that name was familiar to Charlie, for he and Vicky had been pals some years before.

"What-ho, Charlie boy!" Vicky greeted our hero when he went 'behind the scenes' during the interval. "Got something on your mind—besides your hat?" he added with a grin.

"As a matter of fact, I have, Vicky," Charlie confessed. "And I think you can help me."

Over a strong cup of coffee, he told his ventriloquist friend about Auntie Rosie and Walter

Winklepin, and in next to no time they had cooked up a plot which they hoped would make the Winklepin pest wish he had taken a slow boat to China!

"The one thing we need is an unfriendly sort of old codger who will tell Winklepin where he gets off," Charlie concluded.

"And I know the very chap . . . Colonel Firebrand!" said Vicky with a grin.

After the rest of the show, Charlie took Vicky back to Auntie Rosie's house. In the best of spirits they awaited the home-coming of Walter Winklepin. Before he had time to go up the stairs to his own room the telephone in the hall rang . . . or at least, that's what it seemed to do.

Actually, it was Vicky who made the bell-ringing sound!

You see, being a ventriloquist, Vicky could 'throw his voice' at any person or object and make any desired sound seem to come from that person or object.

At the moment, the door of Auntie's parlour was open, for she hurried out to answer the telephone. (Even she was deceived by the realistic bell-ringing sound made by clever Vicky!)

"Hello! Is Mr. Walter Winklepin there, please?" asked a waffly kind of voice over the telephone.

"Yes. He has just come in," answered Auntie. "What name shall I give him?"

"This is Colonel Firebrand speaking," came the same waffly voice from the ear-piece of the telephone.

Even Charlie, standing just inside the open parlour door, found it difficult to realise that the voice really came from Vicky. He certainly was a super ventriloquist.

Hearing his own name mentioned, Walter Winklepin promptly snatched the telephone from Auntie's hand. He knew Colonel Firebrand was a big shot in the town, and he fairly swelled with pride as he listened to what "the Colonel" had to say.

"I say, Mr. Winklepin," waffled the fake voice from the 'phone, "I'm having a party up at my house tomorrow night. I've heard that you are a magnificent trombone-player, and perform in a band."

"Th-that's right, Colonel," gulped Winklepin, trembling with excitement.

"Could you bring your band round to my party tomorrow night, Mr. Winklepin?" the waffly voice asked. "And give a special trombone solo?"

Charlie and Vicky and Auntie saw the nasty lodger's face turn purple with excitement.

"Why, y-yes, of course, Colonel!" he gasped. "Do you want me and the band to play for dancing or . . ."

"No, I want you to serenade my guests, just to give them a happy surprise," the 'Colonel' replied. "Eight o'clock suit you, Mr. Winklepin? Rightio! I'll pay you well. Start playing outside my house just after eight. Good-bye."

Charlie, Vicky and Auntie had swiftly slipped back into the parlour by the time Walter Winklepin replaced the telephone-receiver. He simply couldn't contain his excitement. He had to broadcast his sudden fame, and as he burst into Auntie's parlour he babbled:

"Did you hear that? Colonel Firebrand has asked me to take my band up to his big house tomorrow night . . . to play for him at a party! And I'm to play a special trombone solo! What do you think of that, you silly old woman?" he added rudely to Auntie. "You'll be sorry you tried to stop me practising my trombone when I'm in the 'big time'."

He gave Charlie and Vicky a sneering superior sort of grin, then turned back to the telephone and picked it up.

"Now I'm going to 'phone the other three chaps I shall take with me tomorrow night," he said. "Pete plays the saxophone, Derry plays the drums, and Sid's my trumpet-man."

Then, without asking Auntie's permission, Winklepin started ringing up his pals and engaging them to play, with him, at a "swell party" tomorrow night.

What a Party!

You can guess where Charlie and his clever pal Vicky the ventriloquist went just before eight o'clock the following night . . . Grey Gables, the big home of Colonel Firebrand!

"This is it," grinned Vicky, pausing near the big open gateway. "Do you think Walter Winklepin and his three pals will turn up as arranged?"

"You bet they will!" replied Charlie. "That super pest has been playing his trombone all afternoon. The landlord came to worry Auntie Rosie again today about the noise annoying the neighbours. He said: 'Either *you* get rid of your lodger, or I shall have to turn you out!'"

"Right! Then Winklepin has got to go!" said Vicky, firmly. "Sh!" he added. "I can hear voices! It's them!"

Sure enough Walter Winklepin was approaching with his band!

When the four-man band showed up out of the gathering dusk Charlie and his pal were hidden in the thick hedge.

"Well, this is it, boys!" Walter Winklepin said to his three companions. "Come up the drive near to the front door. That's about right. Now remember, we've got to give 'em all we've got."

"And what's Colonel Firebrand going to

pay us, Walter?" asked the trumpeter.

"Plenty!" said Winklepin, confidently. "He didn't say just how much, but believe me, we're in the money tonight!"

Peering from the hedge, Charlie and Vicky saw the four prepare to play their instruments. Then at a signal from Walter Winklepin, the band struck up.

What a row they made!

"If this doesn't annoy Colonel Firebrand, nothing ever will!" chuckled Charlie to his pal.

"And he didn't ask for it, either . . . although Winklepin imagines he did!" laughed Vicky. "Oho! Here comes trouble!"

His last words were prompted by the sudden opening of the front door of Grey Gables.

"What do you think you are doing in my private driveway?" thundered Colonel Firebrand. "STOP! AT ONCE!"

"B-b-but, Colonel . . ." he started to falter.

"Don't you dare address me, you noisy vagabond!" yelled Colonel Firebrand, shaking his fist under Walter's long nose. "What is the meaning of this hideous noise?"

"It isn't a hideous noise! It's MY BAND playing!" retorted Walter Winklepin, stirred to anger by the Colonel's contemptuous remarks.

"Don't bandy words with me!" barked Colonel Firebrand.

"But you engaged us to play outside your house . . . to serenade your party guests!" faltered Walter, beginning to wonder if he had had a bad dream.

"Party? Guests? What are you blithering about, you noisy nincompoop?" waffled the irate old warrior. "There is no party and I have no guests! Don't try to trick me with such a pack of lies! Take *that*!"

He snatched the trombone from Winklepin's hand and bent it over his head.

"Now be off, all of you, before I call the police!" concluded the Colonel.

Walter Winklepin was bewildered as well as bruised. And he got plenty of bruises from his three pals when they had all retreated down the drive of Grey Gables.

"Well, when do we get our pay?" one demanded, glaring angrily at Walter Winklepin. "You engaged us to play at a party . . . remember? Right! Pay up!"

"Yes—*pay up*!" chorused the other pair, threateningly.

"Oh, get lost!" retorted Winklepin, losing his temper. "I didn't get paid, so you don't either!"

"That's what *you* think!" cried an ex-pal, swinging a punch to Walter's nose. "That's a first instalment of *your* pay!"

The others joined in. They gave the pest a really rough time, and when they left him in the hedge, with his trombone wrapped round his neck, he had also been relieved of all his money. The band had taken their pay!

Needless to say, there was no more noise from Auntie Rosie's house to annoy the neighbours after that night; and when Auntie asked for her rent—and Walter Winklepin hadn't any money!—he had to go.

THE END

As Charlie and Vicky watched, the Colonel brought Winklepin's musical career to a head.

Charlie Chaplin in Scene Stealer!

FUNNY! NO-ONE ABOUT! LOOKS LIKE THERE ARE ALL KINDS OF VACANCIES HERE!

JUST SIT DOWN HERE AND WAIT, I SUPPOSE!

BUT THEN...
'ERE! WHAT'S THAT TRAMP DOING IN MY CHAIR?

UGH! TAKE THAT! YOU IMPOSTER!
THUD!

THAT'S GIVEN HIM THE BOOT! NOW, LET'S HAVE YOU, YOU 'ORRIBLE LOT! ALL ACTORS ON...!

WHUMP!
AAAGH!

HEE, HEE! SERVES THE OLD FOOL RIGHT!
POMPOUS TWIT!
WHO THE... WHAT THE...?

HIM! GET HIM OUT OF HERE!

I NEVER WANT TO SEE THAT HORRIBLE LITTLE MAN AGA...

...AAAAAIN!

GOOD 'UN, LITTLE MAN!
HE'S HAD THAT COMIN' TO HIM!
OOER!
WHY, IF I CATCH YOU...!

NO! WAIT A MINUTE! SO YOU WANT TO BE IN FILMS, EH? WELL, I'VE GOT JUST THE ROLE FOR YOU!
ER, YOU HAVE?

OH, YES! YOU'LL REALLY GO WITH A BANG! TEE, HEE!

IN YOU GO! NOW YOU JUST WAIT IN THERE!
OOH!
RIGHT, EVERYONE IN POSITION. READY TO ROLL..!
THEN, LATER...
RRRING!
CUT! OKAY! EVERYONE! TEN MINUTES TEA BREAK!
MEANWHILE, INSIDE THE CANNON...
TEA BREAK! RIGHT, I'M COMING OUT FOR A BREATHER! THIS FILMING LARK'S TOUGHER THAN I THOUGHT! I THINK I CAN GET OUT BY OPENING THE DOOR AT THE END!
AH! THAT'S BETTER!
BUT...
I WONDER HOW THAT LITTLE FOOL'S GETTING ON IN THERE? CAN'T WAIT TILL THE NEXT SCENE WHEN I *FIRE* HIM! HEE, HEE!
FUNNY! CAN'T SEEM TO SEE HIM!

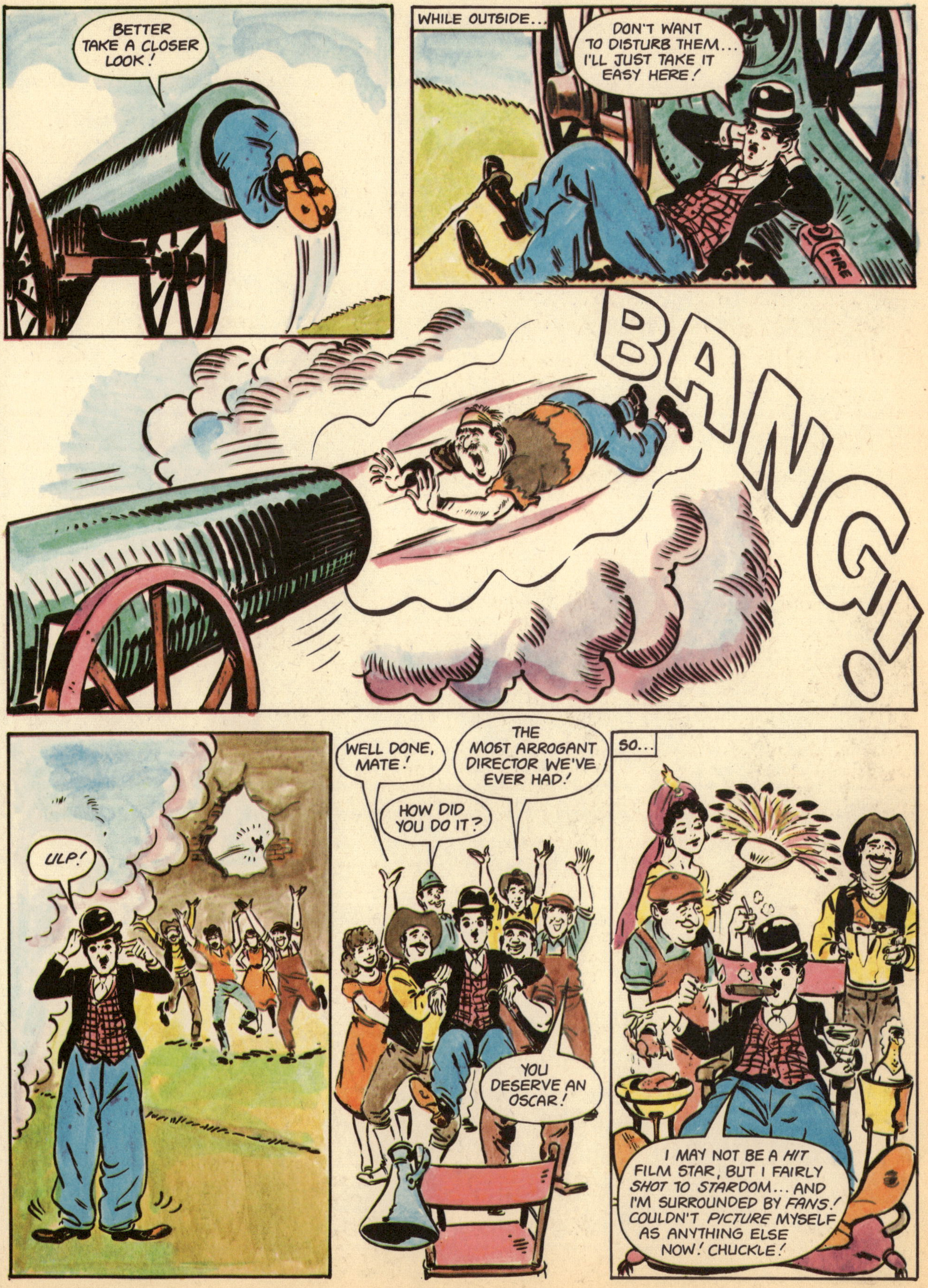

BETTER TAKE A CLOSER LOOK!

WHILE OUTSIDE...

DON'T WANT TO DISTURB THEM... I'LL JUST TAKE IT EASY HERE!

FIRE

BANG!

Charlie Chaplin in

SAFARI SO GOOD

PUSH OFF, YOU MEAN!
SWOOSH!
EEK

FUNNY! THE SKY LOOKS CLEAR ENOUGH! MUST'VE BEEN ONE OF THE TROPICAL STORMS! GOT TO EXPECT SUCH THINGS OUT HERE, I SUPPOSE!

AH! THOSE BUSHED MOVED! MUST BE SOME GAME AT LAST!

BETTER JUST GIVE 'EM A WARNING BLAST TO BRING 'EM OUT INTO THE OPEN! PUT ME STICK DOWN, AND...!

OOOUCH!
BANG!

THAT CERTAINLY BACKFIRED ON ME! EEK! THEY WEREN'T ANIMALS... BUT CANNIBALS! AND THEY LOOK REALLY WILD!

O-OH! N-N-NO! I-I J-JUST DROPPED IN, M-MISTER CANNIBAL..!
...I-I'LL B-BE OFF NOW!
GUGGLE! WOFFLE!
PERHAPS I'LL BE ABLE TO ESCAPE UP...!
BUT...
SWISH
SNAP!
WHOEEE!
OOOOWW!
GOT IT!

THERE! SHOULD BE SAFE UP HERE... WHAT AN ATTRACTIVE TREE *THAT* IS! I'LL CLIMB ON TO IT!

WOW! WHAT A SMOOTH TREE THIS IS...!

BUT...
H-HEY! THE TREE'S *MOVING*!

STOP!...STOP! *PUT ME DOWN*!

IT'S NOT A *TREE* AT ALL...IT'S A *GIRAFFE*!
THE GIRAFFE DULY OBLIGED!
WHEEEE!

SPLASH!

I CAME GAME HUNTING... GULP... NOT FISHING!

BAH! C-CROCODILES! AND IT LOOKS AS THOUGH I'M THE BAIT!

GASP! NEARLY SAFE!

BUT...
UGGLE-GLUG!
OH, NO! THEM AGAIN!

THERE'S ONLY ONE THING FOR IT... RUN!

BUT...
WHOOSH!
GNNN!
TWANG!

AND...
OOGOO! YUGGLE!
L-LET ME GO! I'VE COME HERE TO HUNT GAME...NOT YOU!
YUM!
YUM, YUM!
YUM, YUM, YUM!
THEY'RE NOT PLAYING THE GAME... I HOPE IT'S NOT DINNER TIME YET!
BUT...
IT IS! THAT'S ENOUGH PEPPER! IT ALWAYS MAKES ME WANT TO... AAAA...
CHOOO
THAT'S IT... I'VE HAD ENOUGH... I'M GOING BACK TO ENGLAND! HEY! WAIT FOR ME!
THAT'S THE LAST TIME I PLAY ANY BIG GAMES IN AFRICA!

Charlie Chaplin in Sleep Walking

THUD!

SCREEECH!

ZZZZ

CLUNK!

AAAAGH! WHAT'S HAPPENED? IT'S ALL GONE DARK!

OOOOCH!
WHACK!

HONK-
HONK!

LOOK OUT, YOU FOOL!

KRASH!

CHARLIE WAS SOON HEADING FOR OPEN COUNTRY...
ZZZZZZZZ

COME BACK 'ERE, YOU-YOU SHEEP STEALER!
BAAA!
CREAK!
BAAA!
CREAK!

BUT THEN...
MOOOO!

BOIIIING
?
THUD!

TWIT-TWIT!

URGH!

COME BACK HERE, YOU!... AND KEEP AWAY FROM MY...

WHEEEE!

GLUG!... GLUGGLE!
RIIIP!

A DRIPPING AND TORN CHARLIE WAS SOON HEADING BACK TO TOWN...

ZZZZZ

BZZZ!

SMASH!

AND FINALLY AT 5·30 A.M...

ZZZZZ!

Charlie Chaplin in

CLASSROOM CAPERS

I SUSPECT THIS SILLY FELLOW WAS THE CULPRIT!

CHARLIE'S FORTUNES WERE SEE-SAWING! ONE MINUTE HE WAS DOWN . . .

. . . THE NEXT UP!

WOW! WHAT SORT OF SCHOOL LESSON HAVE I BEEN LET IN FOR?

WHEN THE HEAD AND TEACHER TANNEM CAME IN, THE BATTLE STOPPED . . .

TUT-TUT! THESE BOOKS MUST BE REPAIRED BEFORE YOU CAN STARTA LESSON, MR. TANNEM!
OH DEAR! HOW ANNOYING!

CHARLIE BOY, YOU'VE GOT TO GET OUT OF HERE! THERE'S NO FUTURE FOR YOU IN A CUPBOARD! BUT HOW?
CHARLIE'S PLEA WAS SOON ANSWERED...
BONK!
GOSH! THIS ISN'T MY LUCKY DAY!
A REEL OF STICKY-TAPE! THAT'S THE VERY STUFF WE NEED TO REPAIR THE SCHOOL BOOKS!
HOPING TO GET INTO THE HEAD'S GOOD BOOKS, CHARLIE OFFERED HIS SERVICES...
LET ME REPAIR THEM FOR YOU!
BUT CHARLIE SOON FOUND IT WAS A STICKY BUSINESS!
NEXT MOMENT...
INK
INK
GLOOP! ULP!...
...HAS NIGHT FALLEN?

WHAT IS THE MEANING OF THIS?
IT'S THE GUM, CHUM! CAN'T GET FREE OF THE STUFF! BUT I'M TRYING!
WHOEVER GOT ME INTO THIS MESS? I CAN'T STICK IT MUCH LONGER!
BUT NOW WE'VE GOT NO BOOKS AT ALL!
HE HASN'T MENDED THEM! HE'S TORN THEM ALL UP!

SELDOM HAD THE DEAR LITTLE BOYS HEARD THEIR HEADMASTER UTTER SUCH SWEET AND COMFORTING WORDS . . .
DUE TO THE LOSS OF ALL YOUR BOOKS, I DECLARE THE SCHOOL CLOSED!
CHEERS FOR GOOD OLD CHARLIE! HE GOT US ALL A HOLIDAY!
DID I REALLY? WELL, FANCY THAT!
THE END

DEAR ME! I DON'T UNDERSTAND THEM!
HURRAH! HURRAH! HURRAH!

Charlie Chaplin in SUPER SALESMAN

BUT WHEN CHARLIE GAVE A DEMONSTRATION...
GRRRAGH!
OH DEAR! IT'S SPRUNG A LEAK!

TRY TO SELL YOUR RUBBISH SOMEWHERE ELSE!

FURTHER ALONG THE STREET...
OOH, NASTY!

CHARLIE QUICKLY SAW THE CHANCE OF A QUICK SALE...
WHERE AM I?
HERE YOU ARE, SIR— JUST WHAT YOU WANT! A MAP OF THE TOWN!

FUNNY MAN, EH? GET LOST!
YOWCH!

CHARLIE DIDN'T GIVE UP EASILY...
I MUST TRY TO SELL SOMETHING ELSE!

MADAM, I HAVE HERE THE VERY THING YOU NEED FOR YOUR BUSINESS ... A TAPE-MEASURE! SEE...
...SEE HOW FAR IT STRETCHES!
WHAT A PITY! OUR CHARLIE STRETCHED THINGS A BIT TOO FAR...
HOW DARE YOU MEASURE MY NOSE!
EEEEK!
OOPS! WHAT'S HAPPENING TO ME?
CHINA DEPARTAMENT
HELP! STOP ME, SOMEONE! I'M BEING KIDNAPPED!

OOH! WHAT HAPPENED?
GRRR! I KNOW WHAT'S GOING TO HAPPEN!
GET OUT AND STAY OUT!
I DON'T SEEM TO BE A VERY POPULAR SALESMAN!
OOOOO
AN ALARMING THOUGHT STRUCK CHARLIE... JUST AFTER HE HAD STRUCK THE PAVEMENT!
OOH...
...I'VE LEFT MY BAG OF SAMPLES IN THE STORE! I MUST GET IT!
HE ISN'T THERE... BUT MY BAG IS! I MUST CREEP IN AND GET IT!
GOT IT! MY LUCK'S CHANGED!
JUST THEN...
WHAT THE..?

THE MAN BEHIND THE WHISKERS WAS AS FALSE AS THEY WERE . . .
I'M OFF!

STOP THAT MAN!

CHARLIE IMAGINED THE WARNING SHOUT REFERRED TO HIM . . . AND DIDN'T STOP TO HOLD THE SWING-DOORS OPEN FOR ANYONE!

YOU'VE CAUGHT HIM!

SO, CHARLIE HAD MADE A HIT AT LAST . . .
FIFTY THOUSAND FOUNTAIN-PENS, FIVE HUNDRED MAPS, A THOUSAND TAPE MEASURES, ETC, ETC, ETC.
WHAT AN ORDER!

HOW'S THIS FOR AN ORDER?
GEE! WHAT A SUPER SALESMAN YOU ARE!
THE END

Charlie Chaplin in

SELF DEFENCE

GOODIE! THEY'RE JUST GOING IN!
LOOK WHO'S ARRIVED!
COME ON, SLOWCOACH! MISS THE FIRST BUS, DID YOU!
BUT IT WAS NOT TO BE CHARLIE'S DAY!
THAT'S ALL! FULL UP!
HEE, HEE! THERE'S ALWAYS THE NEXT PERFORMANCE, MATE!
BAH! WHAT A 'PERFORMANCE'!
BRRR! WHAT A WAIT ...
NEXT PERFORMANCE IN 2½ HOURS
... STILL, AT LEAST I'LL BE FIRST IN NEXT TIME! NO-ONE'S GOING TO PUSH PAST ME AGAIN!
AND 2½ HOURS LATER ...
RIGHT, SIR, THIS WAY! THEY'LL BE COMING OUT IN A MINUTE!
THEN...
AAAAAAAH!
TRUNDLE!

BUT SOON . . .

LEARN TO LOOK AFTER YOURSELF! JUDO INSTRUCTION

COO! THAT'S JUST WHAT I NEED!

SO . . .

OH, YES! I'LL LEARN ALL I NEED TO KNOW IN HERE . . . WHOOPS!

THWACK!
GNNN!
YOU DID THAT INTENTIONALLY! YOU'RE FOR IT NOW...
HUH! I'LL TAKE YOU ON ANY DAY!
I'M GOING TO 'TAKE CARE OF MYSELF' AND GET OUT OF HERE...
AAAAAH!
EEE-EEE!
...WHILE THOSE TWO 'BELT' EACH OTHER!
KARATE CLUB
PHEW! THAT'S ONE KIND OF SELF DEFENCE I CAN DO WITHOUT! HELLO! WHAT'S THIS?
NEW MEMBERS WELCOME, EH! NOW THIS COULD BE MORE ME!
NEW MEMBERS WELCOME
AND...
YAAAAAEE!
BRAVO!
WELL DONE!
CRUMBS! THAT WAS EFFECTIVE! HE MADE IT LOOK EASY, TOO!
AH TANK YAH! VOULD AN HONOURABLE GENTLEMAN LIKE TO TRY...
SURE! I'LL HAVE A GO!

SO...
EEE-OOOO-UMMM-AAAH...
BUT...
OUCH!
WHAEEEE!
WHOOPS! I'VE REALLY DROPPED A BRICK THIS TIME!
AAA-AAAH!
SWOOSH!
OOER! I'D BETTER KARATE HERE—FAST!
SUPPOSE I'LL JUST HAVE TO GO ON BEING MY USUAL MEEK, PITIFUL SELF!
WAIT A MINUTE! THAT COSTUME GIVES ME AN IDEA!
AND, TEN MINUTES LATER...
AH! NOW I FEEL TWICE THE MAN I WAS!

SO THERE YOU ARE!
VAIT TILL VEE'VE FINISHED VIV YOU...
HUH! YOU WON'T HURT ME!

OUCH!
AAAGH!
HELLLP!
HEE, HEE! I'VE REALLY KNOCKED 'EM OUT NOW!

THEN...
ER... EXCUSE ME ... STAND BACK...
YOU MUST BE JOKING, MATE!
IT'S THAT WEAKLING AGAIN!

OUGH!
AAAGH!
GERROFF! EEK!

LATER, AT HOME...
BETTER TAKE OFF MY NEW SUIT BEFORE I HAVE A WASH...
...DON'T WANT IT TO GO RUSTY!

THAT SORT OF SELF DEFENCE 'SUITS' ME... IT'LL STAND UP TO ANYONE! HEE, HEE!

OO! MY ACHING BACK...
MY STIFF LEGS!

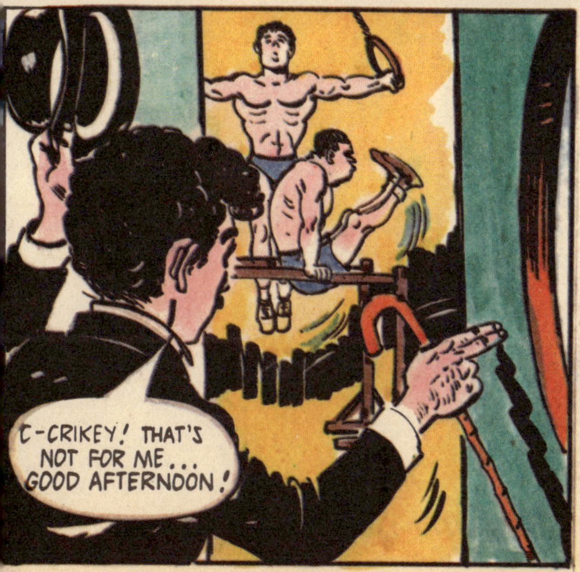

AND...
LOOK, LADS! WE'VE GOT A NEW MEMBER!
HAA, HAA! WHAT A WEAKLING!
HE DOESN'T LOOK FIT FOR ANYTHING!
AT LEAST YOU'LL KEEP US IN FITS OF LAUGHTER!
GRR! I'LL SHOW 'EM!
SO...
THIS WAY, WE'LL TRY WEIGHT-LIFTING FIRST!
OO! I DON'T THINK I'LL BE A HIT WITH THAT!
TWANG!
H-E-A-V-E! THERE! THIS'LL TAKE A WEIGHT OFF YOUR MIND!
YOU'RE A HIT ALREADY, MAKE! HEE, HEE!
BOING!
AND...
PANT! I-PUFF-THINK I'LL DROP THIS-PUFF-IDEA! WHOOPS!
AAAAAAGH!
SO...
STEADY!
WHOA!

OH! ME FOOT! GRR! NOW I'LL PUT YOU THROUGH IT! FOLLOW THEM ON THE HORSE!

SO...
THIS SHOULD BE EASY!

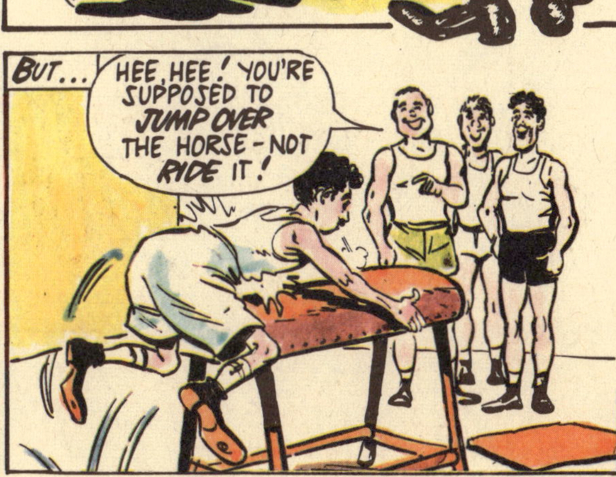
BUT...
HEE HEE! YOU'RE SUPPOSED TO JUMP OVER THE HORSE - NOT RIDE IT!

THIS IS WHAT YOU NEED TO GIVE YOU SPRING, MATE!

THEY'RE NOT GOING TO HORSE ABOUT WITH ME... I'LL SHOW 'EM THIS TIME!

AND...
WHEEEEEE!
DOIIIING!

HELP! GET ME DOWN!

SLIDE DOWN THE ROPE, YOU ASS!

SO...

THIS IS A BIT OF A COME DOWN! HEY! I CAN'T STOP!

KRASH

SO...
EEEEK!

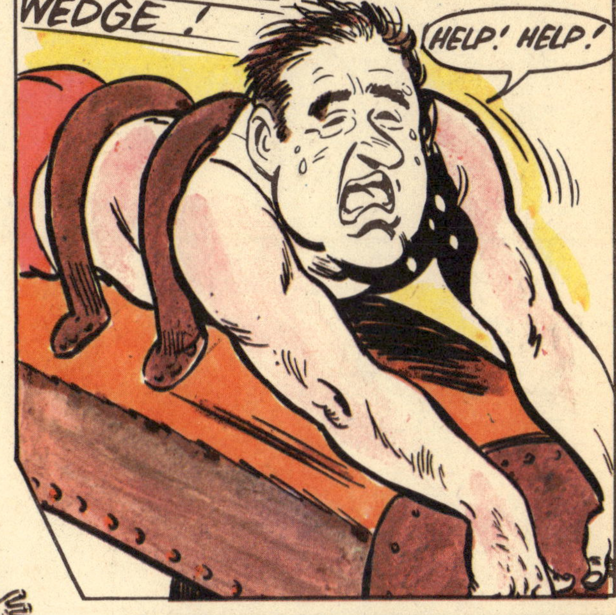
WEDGE!
HELP! HELP!

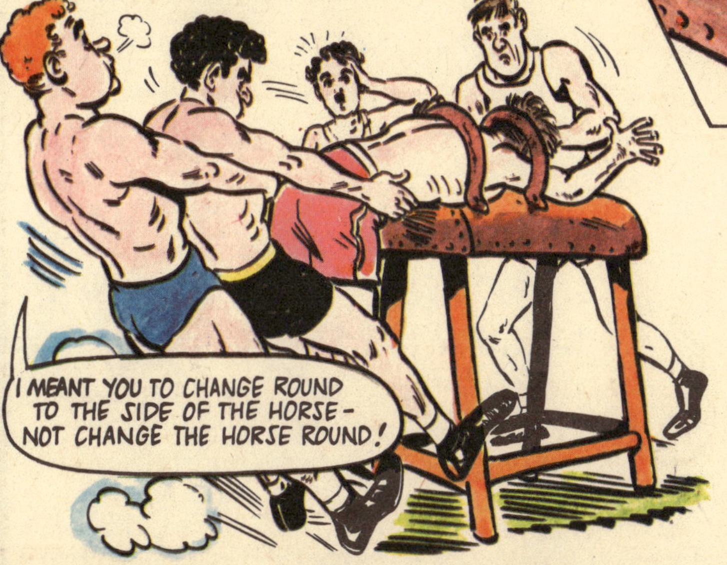
I MEANT YOU TO CHANGE ROUND TO THE SIDE OF THE HORSE - NOT CHANGE THE HORSE ROUND!

NOW JUST SEE IF YOU CAN STAND UNDER THE BEAM IN CASE WE FALL! SURELY YOU CAN'T DO ANYTHING WRONG THERE!
I'M ALL SQUASHED!

SO...
NOW JUST RELAX THERE AND DON'T TOUCH ANYTHING!
I'LL JUST HAVE A LEAN AGAINST THE SIDE!

AT LEAST THEY CAN'T BLAME ME FOR ANYTHING THIS TIME!

BUT...
YIKES! I'M SLIPPING!
SLIP!
AND...
WHOOPS!
EEK!
WOW!
OOH!
MY HEAD!
OUCH!
WHAT HAPPENED?
C-CRIKEY!
JUST FOR THAT YOU CAN CLEAN THE PLACE UP WHILE WE GO AND BATHE OUR HEADS!
EH... Y-YES!
I'LL JUST POLISH THE WHOOPS!
TRIP!
THEN, A FEW MINUTES LATER...
SLIP!
SLIDE!
SLITHER!
WELL, WELL! SEEMS THEY'RE FIT FOR NOTHING! AFTER ALL... BUT I FEEL GREAT! 'BYE ALL!

Charlie Chaplin in

ON THE FARM

YOU CAN START BY HELPING WITH THE APPLE PICKING!
SURE, MISTER FARMER!

SO...
I'LL JUST REACH UP TO THE TOP APPLES...!
OY! BRING THAT LADDER OVER, MATE!

OKAY! ONE LADDER COMING UP!
YAGH!

FANCY TAKING THE LADDER AWAY FROM UNDER HIM!
BUT HE SAID... AND HE SAID...
OUCH!
TROUBLEMAKER! CLEAR OUT OF THE ORCHARD AND GO AND HELP WITH THE HAY-MAKING!

YOU CAN LIFT THE BALES OF HAY ON TO THE TRAILER!
SURE! I SHOULD MAKE HAY ON THIS JOB! HEE, HEE!

BUT...
HERE COMES THE FIRST BAAAAALE!

SPIKE!
BANG!
WHAT WAS THAT NOISE?
I JUST TRIPPED OVER AND... LOOK OUT!
YAAAAGH!
OUCH! OO! EEE!
BAH! SEE IF YOU CAN DO THE SIMPLEST OF JOBS - LIKE COLLECTING THE EGGS!
Y-YES, MISTER FARMER!
SO...
COO! THE FARMER WILL BE PLEASED IF I COLLECT ALL THESE!

CAREFULLY DOES IT!

STEADY AS WE GO! I'M DOING EGGSACTLY AS I WAS TOLD THIS TIME!

BUT THEN...
COCK-A-DOODLE-DOO!
EEEEEK!

AAAAAGH!
OH, NO!

WHAT'S THE IDEA OF SHOWERING ME WITH A BATTERY OF EGGS?
IT WASN'T A JOLK... ER, JOKE, REALLY, MISTER FARMER!

WELL, I'LL GIVE YOU ONE LAST CHANCE! MAKE YOURSELF USEFUL ON THE TRACTOR!
T-TRACTOR? BUT I CAN'T...

...DRIVE A TRACTOR!
VERUUUM!
BAAAH!

THE PASTURE WAS NEXT...
OUT OF THE WAY, SHEEP... EEEK!
SMASH!
MOO... MOO!

HEN, IN THE PADDOCK...
BASH!
NEIGH!

AND FINALLY...
WHAM!
TIMBER!
WHY, YOU... I'LL HAVE YOU FOR THIS... HEY! LOOK! THE ANIMALS HAVE STAMPEDED!

BUT...
WELL DONE, M'BOY! YOU'VE BLOCKED THE ENTRANCE AND STOPPED ALL MY ANIMALS FROM ESCAPING! YOU DESERVE A REWARD!
EH?

SO...
WELL, WELL! THAT WAS BY FARM AND AWAY THE BEST DAY'S WORK I'VE DONE! TEE, HEE!

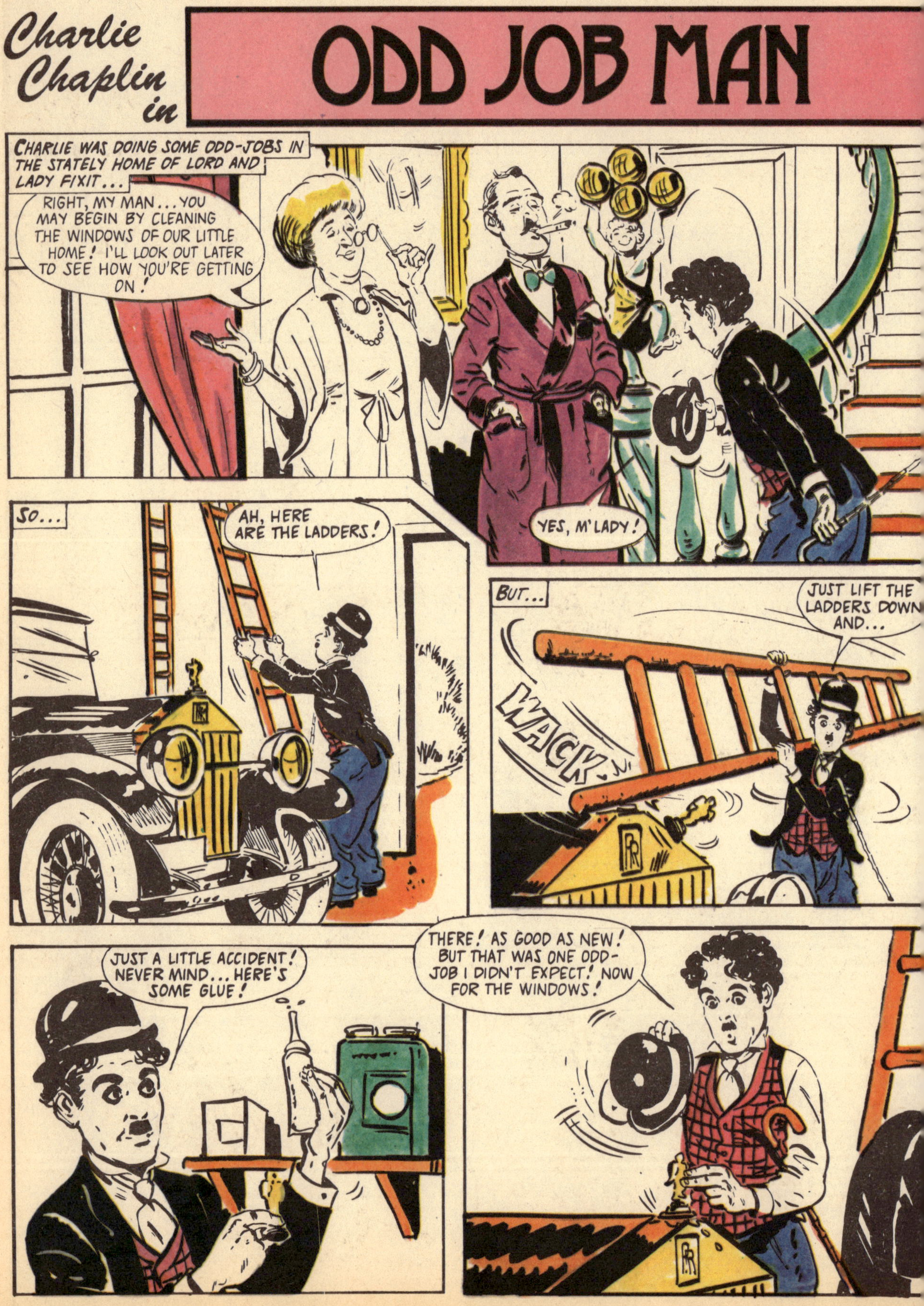

Charlie Chaplin in

ODD JOB MAN

CHARLIE WAS DOING SOME ODD-JOBS IN THE STATELY HOME OF LORD AND LADY FIXIT...

RIGHT, MY MAN... YOU MAY BEGIN BY CLEANING THE WINDOWS OF OUR LITTLE HOME! I'LL LOOK OUT LATER TO SEE HOW YOU'RE GETTING ON!

YES, M'LADY!

SO...

AH, HERE ARE THE LADDERS!

BUT...

JUST LIFT THE LADDERS DOWN AND...

WACK

LADDERS IN PLACE...
BUCKET READY...
NOW UP I GO!

BUT...
HOW ARE YOU... AAAGH!

WELL! WHAT A THING TO HAPPEN!
S-SORRY, M'LADY! THAT WAS A BIT OF A WASHOUT!

CORKS! THE DOGS MUST'VE ESCAPED! HER LADYSHIP WILL BE PLEASED WITH ME IF I TIE THEM UP!

GOOD DOGGIES! YOU JUST STAY THERE WHILE YOUR UNCLE CHARLIE CLEANS THE WINDOWS!

HEN...
HEY! THE LADDER'S SHAKING
SHAKE!

WHEEEE!

CLANG!
OUCH! IT'S ALL GONE DARK!

YOU FOOL! FOR THAT YOU CAN CLEAN OUT THE SEWER! I'LL CLEAN THE WINDOWS MYSELF!

A LITTLE LATER...
PHEW! THINK IT'S TIME I WENT UP FOR AIR! AH! THERE'S A MANHOLE COVER...

BY GAD! THE JOLLY LADDER'S MOVING.
CREEK!

AAAAAARR!
CRIKEY! HIS LORDSHIP'S OVERBALANCED!

YOU BUNGLING IDIOT! GO ROUND THE FRONT. I'LL SEE YOU LATER!
Y-YES, M'LORD!

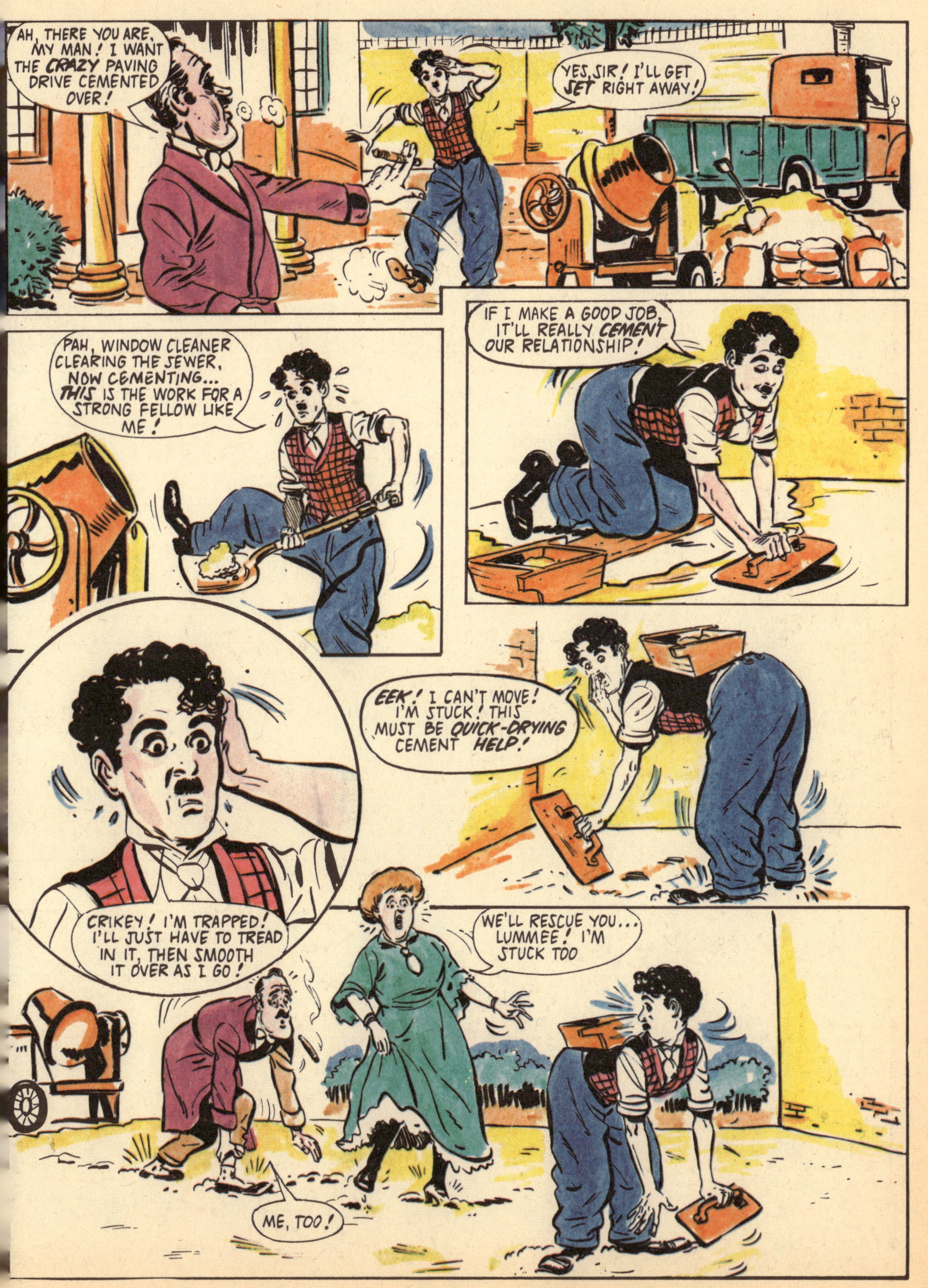
AH, THERE YOU ARE, MY MAN! I WANT THE CRAZY PAVING DRIVE CEMENTED OVER!
YES, SIR! I'LL GET SET RIGHT AWAY!
PAH, WINDOW CLEANER CLEARING THE SEWER, NOW CEMENTING... THIS IS THE WORK FOR A STRONG FELLOW LIKE ME!
IF I MAKE A GOOD JOB, IT'LL REALLY CEMENT OUR RELATIONSHIP!
CRIKEY! I'M TRAPPED! I'LL JUST HAVE TO TREAD IN IT, THEN SMOOTH IT OVER AS I GO!
EEK! I CAN'T MOVE! I'M STUCK! THIS MUST BE QUICK-DRYING CEMENT HELP!
WE'LL RESCUE YOU... LUMMEE! I'M STUCK TOO
ME, TOO!

DON'T WORRY! I'LL SAVE YOU!

WHY! YOU CRAZY FOOL! IT'S JUST THE SAME AS WHEN YOU STARTED NOW!

AND...
CLEAR OFF!
GET OFF OUR LAND!
WHOOPS! LOOK WHERE YOU'RE GOING!
SWAG
BUMP!

AAAAGH!

I'VE COLLECTED UP THE GOODS!
ALL RIGHT, MATE! I'LL COME QUIETLY.
WELL DONE! LOOKS AS IF THIS ROBBER'S SET FOR PRISON!

SO...
GOODBYE! KEEP THE CANDLESTICKS AS A REWARD! YOU'VE SAVED OUR MOST TREASURED POSSESSIONS COME BACK ANY TIME!
HMM! THAT WASN'T SUCH AN ODD-JOB, AFTER ALL! HEE, HEE! WORTH IT'S WEIGHT IN GOLD EVEN!

'I'll win that race,' the horrible Ginger Flinton said, as he stuffed his face with food.

CHARLIE CHAPLIN IN

A RACE AGAINST TIME

Carrying his cane walking-stick in one hand and his famous bowler-hat in the other, Charlie ambled down the main street of Riverpool one sunny morning.

He was impressed by the colourful decorations which hung from lamp-posts and shop-fronts all along the street . . . and our Charlie wasn't vain enough to imagine the decorations were hung there in honour of *his* visit! Not likely!

"Of course, it's the Town Regatta this week!" Charlie reminded himself. "What a bit of luck for me. I shall be able to watch all the races from Welkum Cottage."

Welkum Cottage was a boarding-house, situated beside the tow-path which ran along the river-bank, and it was run by a kindly woman named Mrs. Darling. She was an old friend of Charlie's, and he was on his way there now.

As usual, Charlie found a warm welcome there as soon as he wiped his feet on the 'Welcome' mat.

"Charlie!" whooped the buxom, beaming lady who met him in the hall. "How lovely to see you again! Come right in."

"Hello, Ella," grinned Charlie, giving her a smacking kiss on each of her rosy cheeks. "I wondered if you could put me up for a few days?"

"Put you up?" repeated Ella Darling with a huge smile. "We can put up with you any time, Charlie. Can't we Daphne?" she added to the pretty young girl who came out of the dining-room at that moment.

"Oh, how super to see you, Charlie!" Daphne greeted him. "Course we can put you up. You'll be able to see the Regatta . . . and Robin win!" she added.

It was later, during the evening meal, that Charlie was introduced to Robin Barlow by Daphne. He was a nice young fellow. They sat chatting about rowing.

"Not that I know much about rowing," Charlie admitted. "But you look as if you've got what it takes."

There was loud snort of contempt . . . and, needless to say, it didn't come from Robin. It was a red-headed chap at the next table who made the noise.

"What's that supposed to mean?" Charlie asked him, taking an instant disliking to the snorter.

"It means you must be lame in the optics if you really think young Barlow's got a chance in Saturday's big race!" replied the red-head, nastily. "P'raps he's forgotten to mention—I'M in the race! Makes a difference, doesn't it?"

Robin Barlow gave Charlie a wink.

"This is Ginger Flinton, Charlie," he said by way of introduction. "If we both get through our races on Friday we shall be rivals in the final on Saturday."

"You want to watch out for him," Charlie warned Robin as they finished their meal together. "He's a nasty piece of work."

"Oh, he can't do me any harm," grinned Robin.

But that's where he was wrong. Next morning, when Robin took his light single-seater racing skiff out on the river and started to pull up-stream there was a sudden—CRRR-ACK! and the young sculler fell over backwards and over-turned.

Charlie and Daphne watched anxiously until Robin was seen to have righted his light racing boat and was propelling it towards the river bank as he swam behind it, unharmed.

"Let's have a look at that oar that broke in two, Robin," said Charlie when the young sculler had clambered on to the landing-stage.

A swift examination of the broken oar confirmed Charlie's suspicions.

"Look, Robin," he said, holding the two pieces of oar, "that's no clean break. It was already *sawn* more than half-way through! Someone doesn't like you—much!"

From that time, Charlie kept a sharp eye on him: and he felt that the danger from Robin's red-haired rival had increased when, on the Friday afternoon, both Robin and Ginger won their races in the semi-final events.

"Well, now the final has to be decided between Robin and Ginger Flinton tomorrow," smiled Charlie when he was talking to Daphne that evening.

"Yes," she said. "Isn't it exciting? I'm sure Robin will win, Aren't you?"

Charlie said "Yes", and to himself he added: "But I'm going to make doubly sure he isn't cheated out of a fair chance!"

Still suspicious of Ginger Flinton, Charlie followed him out of Welkum Cottage after dinner that night. Keeping out of Ginger's sight, Charlie trailed him across two meadows and he was beginning to think he was wasting his time when . . . Ginger nipped into a derelict cottage.

"What's he gone in there for?" Charlie asked himself.

He soon learned part of the answer. Ginger Flinton had gone into the empty cottage to fetch something. It was a bulky object which he had evidently hidden there in readiness for what he planned to do this night.

Ginger now retraced his footsteps some of the way, and then turned off down a lane which brought him to the river. His destination proved to be the boat-house . . . the place where all of the rowing-boats were stored for the morrow's Regatta Finals.

When Ginger risked switching on a small light, Charlie saw what it was he had brought from the cottage. It was a small electric-motor with a metal propeller attached to it.

"So that's it!" gasped Charlie. "I thought he might be going to do something to damage Robin's racing-boat. But he isn't. He's fixing that little electric-motor to the bottom of his *own* boat! So, instead of having to row hard against Robin, all Ginger will have to is *pretend* to be rowing . . . and the electric-motor and propeller will do the rest for him! What a crafty one he is!"

When Ginger had finished fixing the electric-motor to the bottom of his boat he switched out the light and crept out of the boat-house . . . grinning like a Cheshire-cat as he thought how he was going to score a tricky win next day.

But he reckoned without our Charlie. Charlie knew how to use a screwdriver and a spanner just as well as Ginger did. And when Charlie left the boat-house half-an-hour later he wore an even more expansive grin.

"Do you think it will be a close race, Charlie?" Daphne asked him as they stood in the crowd, waiting for the starter's pistol to sound.

"I think it may be, for a little way," smiled Charlie. "Then there will be a big surprise."

How right Charlie proved to be!

When the race had started, both young scullers strove hard to take the lead. The four oars flashed swiftly through the sunlit water, and for nearly half of the distance neither Robin or Ginger managed to gain much of an advantage.

Then the cheers of the crowd suddenly increased. Robin was seen to surge past his rival. In moments he had gained a whole length lead . . . and he was still putting on the pressure.

Thanks to Charlie, Ginger Flinton was on his way back...but not in the way he hoped.

"He's winning! Robin's winning!" cried Daphne.

"And now for the big surprise!" chuckled Charlie.

For he—and only he—knew exactly what was happening in Ginger Flinton's boat at that moment. Desperate to beat Robin by foul means now he had failed to beat him fairly, Ginger jabbed his right foot down hard on a small electric switch.

This operated the electric-motor and propeller which he had secretly fitted under his boat during the night.

"Now I'll show 'em how to beat Robin Barlow!" panted Ginger with a crafty grin.

He expected to feel his racing skiff surge forward without him having to exert himself at all, but nothing of the such-which occurred.

Instead of the boat speeding forward, it went into *reverse*! Ginger looked silly. He didn't know whether he was coming or going . . . until the people on the bank started telling him in no uncertain manner.

"You're going BACKWARDS, Flinton! BACKWARDS! Start rowing!"

Going red in the face, Ginger pretended to row, but of course he now found he couldn't pull *against* the powerful electric-motor beneath his boat! It was sweeping him *down*-stream faster than he was rowing *up*-stream a minute before.

He jabbed his foot on the switch again and again, striving to switch *off* the motor. But he couldn't stop it, . . . Charlie had made quite sure of that. Once it was started there was no stopping it!

Naturally, Daphne and her mother and friends were astonished when they saw Ginger Flinton speeding away in reverse, rapidly widening the gap between himself and Robin Barlow.

"But—whatever's making him go *backwards*?" exclaimed Daphne. "He isn't even trying to row now!"

She was glad to see her boy-friend Robin going away to an easy win, but—like everyone else—she couldn't understand what was happening to Ginger Flinton's boat.

A terrific thunder of cheering went up as Robin passed the winning-post. And, minutes later a roar of laughter was echoed along the river-bank as the spectators saw Ginger Flinton sweep across the river backwards and crash into the Umpire's launch.

It was such a pile-up that Ginger's rowing-skiff broke into several pieces, and as it turned upside-down in the water everybody could see the electric-motor, and the propeller, fixed to the bottom!

And everybody then knew Ginger Flinton to be a twister who had tried to cheat and failed . . . thanks to friend Charlie! ●

1. CHARLIE HAS A NICE PUZZLE TO GET YOUR BRAIN WORKING! ALL YOU HAVE TO DO IS TO WRITE THE NUMBERS IN THE CORRECT BOXES SO THAT THE ARROWED LINES WILL ADD UP TO **22**

4	4	4	4	5	5	5	5
6	6	6	6	7	7	7	7

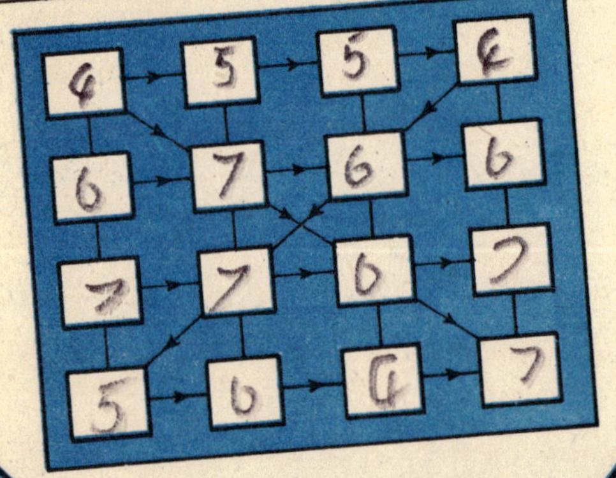

2. HOW MANY KNITTING NEEDLES WHICH ARE PUSHED THROUGH THE CARDBOARD TUBE ARE PERFECTLY STRAIGHT?

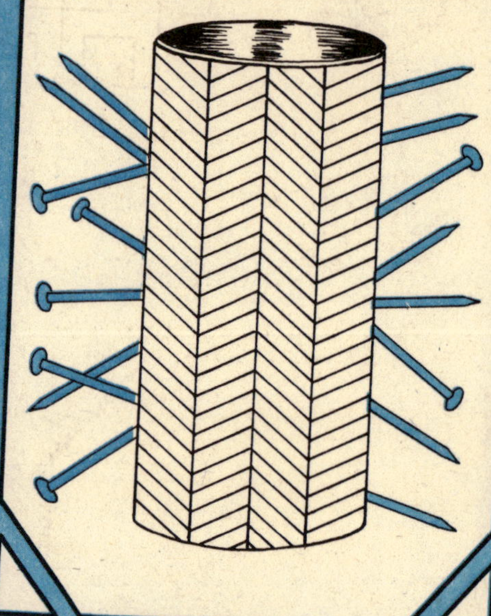

3. SEE IF YOU CAN DRAW SIX STRAIGHT LINES SO THAT EACH LINE PASSES THROUGH THE MIDDLE OF THREE NUMBERS. USE EACH NUMBER ONCE ONLY!

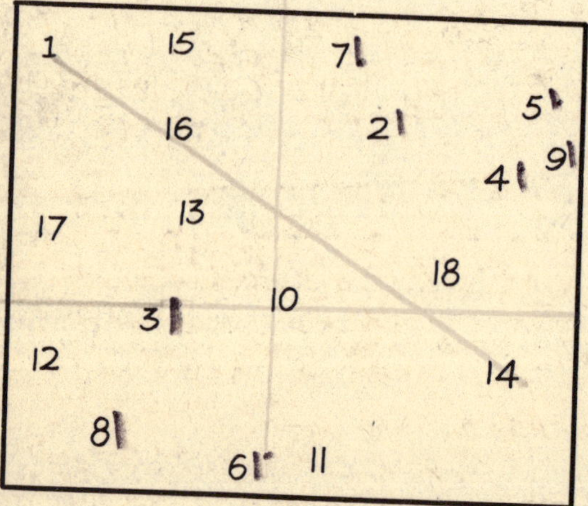

4. CHARLIE'S BEEN BLOWING BUBBLES FOR YOU, NOW HE WANTS YOU TO COUNT THEM!